ANIMAL ATTRACTIONS

ANIMAL ATTRACTIONS

Edited by Diana Edkins

Introduction by Diane Ackerman

Essays by Peter Beard, Virginia Chipurnoi, Kitty Hawks,
Wanda Toscanini Horowitz

Harry N. Abrams, Inc., Publishers
in association with The Humane Society of New York

Editor:
ROBERT MORTON
Designer:
MARIA LEARMONTH MILLER

Library of Congress Cataloging–in–Publication Data
Animal attractions / edited by Diana Edkins ; introduction by Diane Ackerman ;
essays by Peter Beard . . . [et al.].
p.   cm.
Exhibition at Howard Greenberg Gallery in New York on May 25, 1995.
ISBN 0–8109–1959–1
1. Photography of animals. 2. Animals—Pictorial works. 3. Dogs—Pictorial works.
4. Cats—Pictorial works. 5. Pets—Pictorial works.
I. Edkins, Diana. II. Beard, Peter H. (Peter Hill). 1938–
TR727–.A53–1995
779'.32—dc20   94–35232

Published in 1995 by Harry N. Abrams, Incorporated, New York
A Times Mirror Company

Printed and bound in China

Page 2:
BRUCE WEBER
Rowdy and John, Little Bear Ranch, Montana, August 1992. Courtesy of the photographer

PREFACE

Diana Edkins

This has been a wonderful project, allowing me to unearth a wealth of photographic images and thereby opening up a new world. This is not a survey, but an excursion of observations—at once touching, thoughtful, humorous, and full of love.

Animal Attractions is a tribute to those photographers who have focused their visions on the elusive nature of animals. What is so remarkable about this collection is its diversity, the breadth of vision, and its clarity of focus.

I want to thank all the photographers for their wholehearted and enthusiastic participation. Special thanks are due to Janet Borden and Matthew Whitworth, both of the Janet Borden Gallery, New York; Mimi Brown of Art & Commerce, New York; Thomas D. Grischkowsky, Permissions Department, The Museum of Modern Art, New York; Victoria Harris at Laurence Miller Gallery, New York; Margaret Kelly of Pace/MacGill Gallery, New York; Charlotte Kohberger of Mary Ellen Mark's studio, and Lee Marks—all for going that extra mile. True indebtedness lies with Laurence Miller, for his sage advice in the beginning of the project, and both Howard Greenberg and Sarah Morthland for their perfect suggestions at the end. But, of course, the most special thanks go to Virginia Chipurnoi, whose steadfastness and passionate belief in the project were paramount. Without Elizabeth Groves, Sandra DeFeo, Susan Richmond, and Karen Feldman this project would not exist. Last, but not least, thanks to Bob Morton for his experience, patience, and eagle eye.

FOR ALL THE ANIMALS IN THE WORLD, PEACE AND HAPPINESS
—The Buhl Family Foundation

FOREWORD

Virginia Chipurnoi
President, The Humane Society of New York

Our beginning: 1904. Animal activist David Belais founds a society to protect the city's many horses against abuse. Members fight for laws to punish negligent horse owners and place watering troughs in the city's streets and parks. The Humane Society of New York sets standards for quality animal care in the city. As funds allow, the Society expands to include a free medical clinic for cats and dogs.

The Humane Society of New York is an independent, private, non-profit organization. It is run by non-salaried officers and members of a Board of Directors. We have a small paid staff and an enthusiastic group of volunteers. No government funds support the Society, nor are we affiliated with any other hospital or shelter. Through fund-raising, legacies, grants, and donations from our members near and far we support our lifesaving work.

Currently, more than 25,000 animals a year receive quality medical and surgical treatment at low cost from the Society's staff of veterinarians. If we did not exist, most of these animals would be denied medical attention. We are the only source of help for many people who can't afford standard veterinary fees. Each year, we underwrite hundreds of thousands of dollars in emergency care.

Our Adoption Center strives to turn distressed cats and dogs into happy, adoptable pets. Each animal is neutered to help control the enormous problem of overpopulation. Every animal is given medical care, regular exercise, and personal attention until it leaves for a good home. We thoroughly interview each prospective adopter. No animal is released unless we are convinced that it is compatible with its new owner. We are not interested in the number of adoptions, but in the welfare of the animals.

For the animals who depend on the Society—for the hundreds of pets each day who are cleaned, fed, and exercised by a staff that cares, for the dogs, walked daily by volunteers, the cats, whose relaxed forms radiate well-being—the old-fashioned spirit of "home sweet home" is alive and well. For them, The Humane Society of New York is home, for as long as it needs to be.

Eventually there is sadness of parting.

Janise Bogard

So many faces in and out of my life
Some will last, some will just be now and then
Life is a series of hellos and good-byes
I'm afraid it's time for good-bye again.

Peter Wood

They leave us with the sweetness of memories. We are privileged to share their lives.

There is joy in caring for animals, but also great responsibility. The animals have done nothing wrong. Their lives are their own and they are entitled to live them fully, with dignity. Though our work is primarily with city animals, we are concerned with all the creatures that share this earth. If man insists on imprisoning animals, it must be in the most caring fashion that can be provided, and not in the most indifferent manner. Anything else is betrayal.

INTRODUCTION

Diane Ackerman

We see it grazing in a field: some lost version of what we were or who we are—animal. We do not know our future. Animals such as albatrosses and porpoises always seemed to us messengers and portents, full of oracular magic, able to offer us a companionship we crave but somehow cannot give to one another, an antidote to our terrible loneliness in our alabaster cities, a connectedness with our primitive past. We look at them and know they dwell in a realm somewhere between us and our beginnings. We have littered our myths and cities with images of animals, which accompany us throughout our lives; they are the first crib toys we give to our children; women sometimes marry them in fairy tales; we use them as Zodiacal signs to count the hours in our days. We understand how animals fit into the scheme of nature. As for ourselves, we aren't so sure who we are, or where we've come from, and even less what we wish to become.

We are used to having cats and dogs as companion animals, warm-blooded creatures that enjoy affection and some eye contact. They help us bridge that no-man's-land between us and Nature, between apehood and civilization. We are still apes, of course. It is still a wilderness. We attempt to cross it with camera lens or idea, but the deeper we penetrate the frontier the vaster it seems. We long to merge with nature, and yet we also struggle to keep it at arm's length.

But something deep inside us remembers being accompanied by animals. We have worn the same costumes, we have heard the same outcries, we have known the same square-dance in our cells. Their journey is our dance. We adopt pets, and, if a cat sitting on a couch doesn't look or smell exactly like a lion resting at a water hole, well, perhaps it's close enough.

Just as we do with the elements, or with smells, we make animals tidy by putting them on leashes or in zoos. Projecting our values onto them, we give them dishes to eat from, sweaters and rhinestone-studded collars to wear, and we prefer it if they're well behaved.

Inviting them into our homes, we feed and clothe them, as if they were refugees from a war-torn world. No animal is too poor, meek, or humble to receive the haven of someone's love. But they offer us a haven as well. In addition to the incalculable boon of love and companionship, they also provide insights. Through pets, we peer into the lives and ways, joys and desires, habits and obsessions of another species. Amicable aliens, who come from an early chapter in the ongoing memoir of earth, they teach us the many forms that life can take. They connect us to the almost unimaginable phantasm of our origins, when creatures were born with tails, a colossal gift of speed, alert ears that heard what escapes us now, deft noses that read all the fine print in aromas. At times mirroring our actions with startling ease, at others acting out all-too-familiar dramas, they nonetheless differ radically in how they perceive the world, go about solving problems, worry and rejoice. That fascinating difference hints at what it would be like if we were suddenly more—or less—than ourselves. As we usher them into our family and heart, our own eccentricities, no matter how awkward or bizarre, seem all the more endearing. This happens even when we gaze at photographs of animals. A chimpanzee patting its cheeks with its feet—haven't we all longed to be contortionists? William Wegman's infinitely persuadable Man Ray staring at a bust of himself—haven't we all felt the same confused fascination? A mother pig nose-nuzzling her baby—haven't we all lolligagged in that way with our young?

A recent Gallup poll found that fifty-eight percent of American households have pets. Forty percent of the people have dogs; twenty-six percent have cats. But ninety percent of the people said that they regarded their pet as "part of the family," which brought a sense of fullness and completion to their lives. Owning a pet is the single most important factor in the health and longevity of elderly people. Just stroking an animal lowers one's blood pressure. So does just watching it sit. Seeing nature being calm calms us. Most pet fondling takes place unconsciously, the way one's hands absentmindedly stroke each other, or the way spouses press together as they sleep. Soothing, quieting, having a pet lie beside one tranquilizes the nerves. "Companion animals," as they're rather sweetly called, also provide an unflagging friendship and give owners a sense of playfulness and purpose.

The minute a pet enters a household, it joins the family dynamics, and that can be either good or bad depending on the people involved. For example, pets sometimes become the outpatients of a troubled family. When I was growing up, I had a friend, Barbara, whose parents bought a cocker spaniel. They named it Babe, and it became the "good little girl" in their household, as they so often told it, sometimes saying such things to it as: "Here comes your mother, Babe," or "Babe, go to your sister." Barbara's parents quarreled a lot, and they often spoke to one another through the dog. Her father might say something like: "Babe, tell your mother I'm not going to the store, and that's final!" And her mother might answer: "Babe, tell him I'm going whether he likes it or not!" Babe became deeply attached to Barbara's mother, whom she followed like an acolyte from room to room, next to whom she slept in bed every night, and whose absence made her too depressed even to eat. Once, when Barbara's parents were on vacation in Europe, her mother called the dog sitter to make sure Babe was eating all right. If she hadn't been, the vacation would have been cut short.

When it came to looking after Babe, nothing was too much trouble, not even baking her meatloaflike meals. Barbara, on the other hand, was entering puberty, and she and her mother always seemed to be fighting—about her friends, her taste in clothes, her music, her politics, and a hundred other things. Her father worked all day, and came home tired and bad-tempered; except for yelling, he hardly spoke to her at all.

Barbara's mother formed a powerful love for the dog, which loved her back devotedly, wet the floor with rapture whenever she returned home from work, never yelled at her or disagreed with her or confronted her with thorny child-rearing problems, and didn't make complex demands. It was easy to shower affection on the dog, which she kissed and cuddled and groomed, and which, indeed, had become the good little girl in the family. Barbara, Babe's "sister," was relegated to the status of bad little girl. The pet enabled Barbara's parents, who didn't feel comfortable expressing love with one another or with their children, to bestow it on some living thing. This made Barbara feel resentful, as she watched her parents express love for the dog with a generosity they could not seem to muster for her. The dog joined the family, but Barbara felt excluded from it.

People love their pets as children, that is, as specially exempt children. They will never grow to human size, or join in a game of canasta, or pass their college boards, or play saxophone, or refrain from making rude noises when company's around. They are not judged by their potential, not expected to develop, achieve greatness, or fulfill a private fantasy to be a doctor, baseball player, or rock star. They do not disappoint us, scandalize us, or cheat our expectations. We allow them the freedom to be exactly what they are, without worrying about what they must become. We let them live on their own schedule, at their own pace, as we rarely do with real children. And because we expect nothing more, they perpetually please us.

KEITH CARTER
Spotted Horse, Tyler County, 1988. Courtesy of the photographer

JOYCE RAVID
Horse, 1980. Courtesy of the photographer

Cat and Mouse, ca. 1930. Courtesy of Berenice Abbott/Commerce Graphics Ltd, Inc. and Lee Marks

SIDNEY STAFFORD
Dachshunds Stick Together, 1990. Courtesy of the photographer

MARY ELLEN MARK
Project X, 1986. Courtesy of the photographer

Cows, from the series *Le Bestiaire*, 1993. Courtesy Janet Borden Gallery, New York

Siegfried and Roy's White Tiger, 1990. Courtesy of the photographer

ELAINE MAYES
Peacock and Rabbits, Oahu, 1989. Courtesy of the photographer

HORST
Warhol's Dog, 1983. Courtesy of the photographer and HG

Isabella Rossellini's Dogs, 1992. Courtesy of the photographer and HG

CHRIS SCHIAVO
Harley and Friends, 1992. Courtesy of the photographer

Horse from *Manscape with Beasts*, 1986. Courtesy of the photographer

WILLIAM WEGMAN

Man Ray Contemplating Man Ray, 1976–1991. Copyright William Wegman, Courtesy Pace/MacGill, New York

BARBARA NORFLEET
Peaches, 1978. Courtesy of the photographer

JOYCE RAVID
Untitled, 1993. Courtesy of the photographer

ELAINE MAYES

Disappearing Cat Under Hedge, 1977. Courtesy of the photographer

MARY ELLEN MARK
A Passage To Vietnam, 1994. Courtesy of the photographer

Left: ELAINE MAYES
Red on Picnic Table, 1976. Courtesy of the photographer

Smoke et Cigarette: A Champion, 1905. Courtesy: Howard Greenberg Gallery, New York

SET OF TWENTY-ONE HUMOROUS PHOTOGRAPHS
ca. 1910, Courtesy of Gallery 292, New York

CATS

Wanda Toscanini Horowitz

I have loved cats since I was a little girl. At that time I didn't even know why. First of all, I liked their independence, their indifference, which many people resent. This is because people don't talk to cats. They talk to dogs, and to other people, but not to cats. But if you talk to cats they understand and will answer you.

When I married, my husband did not like cats. One night he came to me and said that there was a cat clinging to a window screen on the second floor. The cat had climbed up on an old wisteria plant. I said, "Let the cat stay until tomorrow, and then we will put it back down. In the morning we will bring it downstairs." But in the morning the cat was on the bed. I asked my husband what had happened and he said that the cat had come and kissed his hands. From then on, my husband, who never had cats, would always carry on a conversation with Fussy. We named him Fussy because he was fussy about what he would eat. He knew when it was 8:00 P.M., and would meow for us to come to the kitchen and feed him his chopped liver. That was what he liked. He was orange colored, ginger.

Once, in Connecticut, Fussy disappeared. I jumped into the car, and said, "I am going, Fussy's gone, Fussy's gone." Then I saw him on the roof. Another time the caretaker came and said, "Fussy's on the roof." He was on the roof of the barn that time. It started to rain. I put on my jeans, because I knew that there was poison ivy near the barn. But before I could go out my husband went up on a ladder. I said, "You're crazy. Fussy will come down," and I went to bed. Fussy came down on his own.

Once when Fussy was missing my husband said, "I am not going to give concerts anymore." He was so upset because Fussy disappeared. Fussy was gone for four days. Then I found him in the garden; he needed some time to himself.

One day I was in the garden, and I heard a strange sound. Someone had put into my garden a little kitten. Naturally, I tried to find her a home. She was full of fleas. My husband found fleas in his bed and a friend found fleas on our kitchen floor. We got rid of the fleas, and I found a nice home for the kitten.

One day I was walking outside with my dogs and heard a meowing sound. Under a car was a little black cat. I took him home, and we named him Mini, because he was so small. He did not stay small, however, he grew to be very big. So then we had two cats, Fussy and Mini, and two dogs, Pippo and Lilly, two French Poodles. We were a family.

When I was in the country one night, I went to visit some friends. In their garden, a little gray cat came to me. My friends said that they were going to go to Mexico. So I took the cat and drove home. She was almost like a Russian Blue, gray, very small. Her name was Bigia, which means gray. That was our third cat.

A neighbor of mine loved birds, but she also had a stray cat with long hair. She said, "I cannot keep her any longer because she catches birds." So I took the cat, and then I had four cats and two dogs. I loved all the cats, because when I talked to them they responded. They all lived to be eighteen or twenty years old. Then I lost them.

I began collecting figurines of cats. So there was Mrs. Horowitz, with lots of figurines, paintings, needlework about cats, but no real cats. After I lost all my cats and my two dogs I didn't know what to do. I had always contributed a little to The Humane Society of New York. One day, with my friend, Giuliana, I went to The Humane Society on 59th Street to choose a cat. There was a cat with a lovely face, but she would have been no Miss America because she was fat. The woman there said, "Take this cat, she has a wonderful disposition." The cat was two years old, and had been spayed. She had been living with people who were divorcing. Apparently they yelled at each other all the time and the cat was frightened. The woman said her name was Sam. I said, "What do you mean, Sam? This is a female."

I took her home, but I couldn't get used to her. The cat was extremely frightened. At one point I wanted to give her back. My friend said, "Wanda, don't, this is a wonderful cat."

So we chose a new name. I discovered that her name had been Samantha, but we changed it to Daisy. She was frightened when she came to us because she had lived with two people who were fighting. For one year she never went even so far as from the window sill to the couch. Now, I must tell you, when I am in bed I don't have to call her. I hit my mattress and in two seconds Daisy is there. She puts two paws and her face on the pillow. And she understands everything I say. Now that I am alone, Daisy is really a great company to me. And I must tell you that now again I have a collection of cats. I have figurines and prints and a beautiful painting of white cats in my bedroom, and I have Daisy.

The story is not over, there is another chapter. In 1990 I bought a house in Massachusetts. One day a cat, very beautiful, came toward my house. A friend said, "Please, Wanda, don't feed her." But when I see a stray cat I feed it. Because this cat wanted to be outside, I made a cat entrance in the basement, and she came and went all the time. The cat entrance also led from the basement to the living room. One day the cat came and looked very fat. She was pregnant, and later brought three or four babies and put them under the deck. When they were old enough I brought the mother and babies to the vet to be altered and have shots.

My caretaker loved cats, but was allergic to them. One of the new cats bit him, and he got an infection. The cat cost me more than a thousand dollars. I also had to close the entrance to the cat door because one cat came in and sprayed all over the house. One was picked up by a woman, one disappeared for the summer and came back in January, February, and March. It went into the basement. There was one little one, most beautiful. It would go into the basement. The only one allowed into the living room was the mother—we called her Micetta—who could turn onto her back, and open a door. She spent her nights in the house.

So now I have Daisy, Micetta, and two cats who come and go. Micetta has taken over the house, but at 7:00 A.M. she wakes everybody because she wants to go out. When I say "Mici, Mici, Mici," she comes to me. Micetta sleeps on a white sheet on the corner of the sofa. She brings me presents—mice, a little rabbit, one time a rat. Micetta is true to her instincts.

Daisy does not like to go to the country. If you put her outside she will stay two seconds and run back into the house. In the city she is happy. She has a whole house to herself, and her own toy on the chair. I would like another cat in the city, maybe, but Daisy would not like it. She is happy together with me. I would like a dog, too, not a little one, a big dog, maybe a Labrador.

Why do I love cats? I don't know. There is something very mysterious about them. They are very beautiful. They are amusing. They understand everything. People think they don't understand very much, but I have read books filled with stories about what cats can do. There are people who don't understand cats, but cats understand people.

ANN GIORDANO
Moxie, from the series *Bark*, 1991. Courtesy of the photographer

SYLVIA PLACHY

Indifference, Prague, 1991. Courtesy of the photographer

ELLIOTT ERWITT
New York, 1974. Elliott Erwitt/Magnum

Photographer and Pony, 1950s. Courtesy Howard Greenberg Gallery, New York

Mullinvat—County Kilkenny, Ireland, 1992. Courtesy of the photographer

JANISE BOGARD
Expletive Deleted, 1992. Courtesy of the photographer

New York City, c. 1971. Copyright Helen Levitt, Courtesy of Laurence Miller Contemporary Photographs, New York

LEN JENSHEL
Koh Samui, Thailand, 1984. Courtesy of the photographer

MITCH EPSTEIN
Jaipur, India, 1985. Courtesy of the photographer

Monkeys and Pilgrims, Galta, India, 1978. Courtesy of the photographer

KEITH CARTER

Cutler Family, Houston County, 1988. Courtesy of the photographer

DOGS

Kitty Hawks

It has been noted that of all the living species on earth, the only one that has chosen to love humans is the dog. This is not to say that others—cats, horses, birds, reptiles, hamsters, and others—do not please us with their beauty, their companionship, and often their friendship. I think that much of what we feel in relationships with animals is enormous gratification that these exotic creatures deem us worthy of attention.

The relationship with a dog is entirely different. It is much more a relationship of equals. A dog knows what we are thinking, what we are feeling, what we are wearing, where we are going. Dogs have distinctive personalities. So when we come home to them, we are returning to a soul that knows us, and, best of all, loves us.

I have had two remarkable dogs. Murphy The Dog began life with me as a palm-sized black and white puppy. He came from a pound, and grew to be the size of a small Shetland pony. As is true with many large dogs, he had no sense of his size, often trying to curl up in the lap of an unsuspecting guest. He was an independent thinker with favorite pastimes. Though confined to a generous yard with adequate cool places provided by trees and a patio, he found other ways to cool off. I would often return home to find Murphy calmly swimming laps in the pool. He had humor, intelligence, wisdom, and astonishing gentleness. He is missed by all who knew him.

Earl the Pearl E.T. Smith is not unlike Murphy The Dog in the affection he generates. He, too, began his life in a pound. He was described as "Australian Shepherd Mix/Blue Merle," hence his name. The match between us was his choice. At the pound, I was presented with two dogs and Earlie Bird marched right over and demanded that he be brought home. He has exerted his will ever since.

Strangers cannot enter the house without giving him a dog biscuit, because they are barked at, herded, and pointed at the right cupboard until they understand what they are to do. Earl's toys are chosen deliberately and specifically on the basis of some mysterious canine criterion. It may be the time of day, the toy's shape or sound, who knows what, but clearly some toys are rejected in favor of others. Earl also has his favorite pastimes. One of them is fetching almost anything he can lift. Like Murphy, he enjoys swimming: one day, without warning, he leaped into the fountain of the Metropolitan Museum.

Being part, probably predominantly, Australian Shepherd, Earl carries the breed's best instincts. He has an uncanny sense of geography. One visit to a place and it is permanently etched in his memory. No matter how much time has passed since he's seen it, or whether the place is urban or rural, he will turn toward a doorway or rise to attention when he approaches a place he knows. Familiar places, especially in the country, produce in him a nearly frenzied enthusiasm, not unlike a child's "Are we there yet? Are we there yet?" The difference is that Earl always knows exactly how close we are, and when we have, indeed, arrived.

Earl takes his job of shepherd seriously. When I am alone in the country, although there is plenty of room in the house and plenty of room outside, he is never more than five feet away. When I am not alone, he increases his radius, but he always positions himself to monitor comings and goings. It is not that he lacks independence, but rather that he feels that his presence guarantees absolute safety. His capacity as a guard has somewhat diminished this year (his 13th). His hearing is not quite so acute, nor is his eyesight. I believe that he knows this, and feels guilt and confusion if someone's entrance escapes him. If the person has entered and been embraced, he knows our safety is intact, but usually feels the need to remind us that without his barking we might be dead.

Similarly, Earl seems to hold some of a human's best instincts. He has a sense of direction, a sense of time, a sense of fashion, and a sense of humor. He reminds me of certain

schedules if they are ignored, and he knows the difference between high heels and sneakers, suits and jeans. If alone in the car with his owner, who has a legendary capacity to get lost, Earl knows from the circling and muttering that bearings have been lost, and immediately comes from the back seat to offer comfort and guidance.

All of these traits are apparent to anyone he knows. The affection he generates has resulted in his own correspondence file, including letters and postcards from people all over the country. He has also been invited for long weekends unaccompanied by his owner (I hope not a reflection on how bad my company is but, instead, how phenomenal his is). One of his best friends has a car and a driver. He began quite quickly to associate long, black waiting cars with a great time, and has been seen entering limousines when their doors are opened for passengers by their unsuspecting drivers.

I have often pondered the nature of such life-enhancing souls as Earl, and have concluded that they possess amounts of compassion, sensitivity, intelligence, humor, and affection which most of us can envy. Their spirits are every bit as strong as ours: they are brave, more selfless and trusting, never cynical, always optimistic, and permanently loyal. I cannot imagine a world without such beings. It might be a slight exaggeration to admit to Earl that without him I would be dead, but my life would be dimmer by thousands of watts. Often, relationships are measured by what is added to one's life, and what is taken from it in exchange. A relationship with an animal, and certainly with a dog, is one of mutual addition, with no subtraction—unless you count saying good-bye.

WILLIAM WEGMAN
Earl and Kitty, 1930. Courtesy of William Wegman, Pace/MacGill Gallery, New York and Kitty Hawks

AUGUST SANDER

Forsterkind (Daughter of a forester), Westerwald, 1931. Courtesy of Gerd Sander and The August Sander Archiv, Koln

JEAN BARNARD
The Dog Express, c. 1910. Courtesy Howard Greenberg Gallery, New York

EMMET GOWIN

Barry, Dwayne and Turkeys, Danville, Virginia, 1970. Copyright Emmet Gowin, Courtesy of Pace/MacGill Gallery, New York

Tanjour, South India, 1987. Courtesy of the photographer

DOMINIQUE NABAKOV
Conversation Piece, Les Landes, France, August 1989. Courtesy of the photographer

TINA BARNEY
Mom, I Want a Pony, 1993. Courtesy Janet Borden Gallery, New York

ELAINE MAYES
Boy and Goat, 1989. Courtesy of the photographer

Portrait of Rhonda Cook with Shar-peis, Parrot and Cougar, 1992. Courtesy of the photographer

JESSIE TARBOX BEALS

Judith Anderson with her Great Dane, Rex, ca. 1925. Courtesy Howard Greenberg Gallery, New York

MARY ELLEN MARK
Milos Forman, 1993. Courtesy of the photographer

MARY ELLEN MARK
Welfare Family Ohio, 1989. Courtesy of the photographer

Henry and Katrina, Raymond, New Hampshire, 1993. Courtesy of the photographer

ARTHUR ROTHSTEIN

Boy with Chicken, China, 1946. Courtesy: Howard Greenberg Gallery, New York

KEITH CARTER
Boy with Birds, Hardin County, 1989. Courtesy of the photographer

Larry and C. J. with Miles and Nikita, Brookline, Massachusetts, 1992. Courtesy of the photographer

ROSALIND SOLOMON
Crying Girl, Peru, 1980. Courtesy of the photographer

Laughing Horse, 1980. Courtesy of the photographer

It's quite easy making friends in England

SAGE SOHIER

Agatha, Laura and Squiggy, Rowley, Massachusetts, 1992. Courtesy of the photographer

MARY ELLEN MARK
Help Portrait, 1993. Courtesy of the photographer

A Day in the Life, DITLO, Ireland, 1991. Courtesy of the photographer

Jack Witt, Tyler County, 1987. Courtesy of the photographer

MARY ELLEN MARK
Indian Circus, Fall, 1989. Courtesy of the photographer

Mr. and Mrs. Lubner in bed watching TV, 1981. Copyright William Wegman, Collection of the Center for Creative Photography, Tucson

EVE SONNEMAN
Wendy and her Iguana, 1993. Courtesy of the photographer

Lost Brown Fuzzy Hair Dog, undated. Courtesy Pace/MacGill Gallery, New York

Landscape with Young Boy and Two Dogs, Peru, 1980. Courtesy of the photographer

Lucy in the Snakewoman's House, Louisiana, 1992. Courtesy of the photographer

RALPH GIBSON
Untitled, 1973. Courtesy of the photographer

NAT FEIN
Sharing cabs during New York bus transit strike, c. 1950. Courtesy of the photographer and Armand Rumayor

LAST WORD FROM PARADISE
—ECHOES OF DR. STRANGELOVE

Peter Beard

The ruined wood
We used to know,
Won't cry for retribution—
The men who have destroyed it,
Will accomplish its revenge.

What smart animals fear the most is *us*.

Every four days a million of us are added to the already overloaded Spaceship Earth. Depending on when we agree that early apes like Australopithecus had evolved enough to be called "human"—about three million years ago—it took *that* long—until circa 1850 for our population to achieve one billion...now we add a billion Homo sapiens every decade.

To quote the British medical journal *The Lancet* (September 16, 1990): "If the bomb at Hiroshima had been exploded every day since August 6, 1945, world population would not have stabilized." Our politicians discuss the homeless, rising crime, the drug epidemic, food stamps, urban ghettos, unemployment, racism, domestic violence, police brutality, the Washington Redskins (teaching the young to kill for an inch)...how about some underlying causes?...*expanding* beyond the carrying capacity of the land, mismanagement, neurotic territorialism and the mania for pecking order advancement, selfish animalistic behavior, killing the Redskins, queueing for Concordes, rhinoplasty, liposuction, Lee Nails, distancing ourselves from Nature. First human pollution, then radioactive pollution, sprawling suburbs like deep-rooted cancer, cement condos, the prison system, network TV, the lowest common denominator, Madison Avenue, LeFrak City, Seven Eleven, New Jersey Safari Park, the vari-

ous Simpsons, the cloned Colonel Sanders, plastic wrapping, blue hair, Bigger Burger, and beyond. The Galloping Rot.

In our world if it's close to Nature it's passé, doomed and forgotten—except by the extremists, ecomaniacs, gun toting anti-abortionists, enviro-nazis and worse. Ahhhh—we're surrounded, unartistically painted into a corner. Art and Nature are fine for kindergarten, after that Grow up!— move to Love Canal...be an executive at Exxon...join the World Wildlife Trust or The Humane Society. But demographically speaking, it is very late in the game to be physically or morally *saved* by wealthy, guilt-ridden, sentimental charity drives, fundraising pablum—"bunny hugging" as the wildlife management biologists call it, misleading the directions of conservation. The politics of short term fund-raising—"saving the game"— have consistently failed over many earnest years, plain for all to see—relentless pressure and destruction from us, masters of the reverse Midas Touch, PCBs and acid rain paving the road to Hell...massive denial!...pious Popes...failing in the kind of education which could lead to sustainable survival.

Yes, this could be known as the century when all of us sanctimonious, anthropomorphic, bleeding hearts from Walt Disney country, "man kind" pushed by excessive *densities* and *stress* and innumerable stress-related horrors—all echoes of Dr. Strangelove—hugging darling Dumbo—"buy an elephant a drink"—desperate disillusioned adults displaying infantile regression longing for their nursery pets—obsessive avoidance of their own natural aggressiveness—Sigmund Freud—Charles Darwin—Thomas Malthus—Dr. Norman Borlaug —from the biolabs in Bangladesh to the Calhoun rat study cages in Bethesda, Maryland: "separation of the sexes," "territorial neuroses"—heart disease from stress and pollution, competition from diminishing resources, cancer, HIV, personality disorders, hormone screwups, a sharp decline in tolerable human behavior—Somalia, Rwanda, Zaire, Mozambique, South Africa, Bosnia; and beyond—Hate and Blame—genocide, knife rape, kidnapping, incest, serial killing . . . we are literally going crazy, *breaking the back of Nature*, pressuring, squeezing, forcing our gross intrusion beyond the point of no return . . . e.g. East Africa after a century of missionary manipulations: endless slum squalor, AID and AIDS, lost heritage, lost identity, corrugated iron, crime, pollution, garbage everywhere, tribal clashes, army rule, torture, assassinations, voodoo, overpopulation, unemployment, rape, rap, gangrenous graffiti, occasionally an open air zoo; tourism!—highway robbery. In Africa now the slums are named after us—"Chicago," "Washington, D.C." Benevolent aid workers and the gardeners of Eden have a monopoly of triumphs—"they make a desert and call it peace". . . Brave New World . . . 2001 . . . indefatigable Road Warriors, feasting on Soylent Green after the growth and waste scourge. Slash and burn, destroy and adapt. Refugees scramble for a space niche—frantic well meaning modern day dinosaurs, poised at the edge of the lily pond, begging money for ARF.

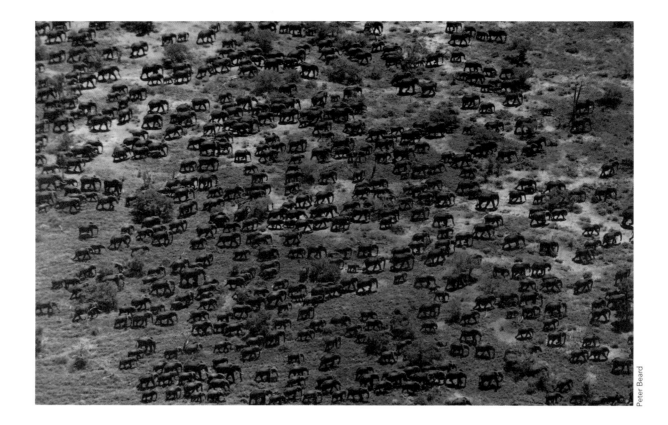

Peter Beard

Surely it is obvious enough, if one looks at the whole world, that it is becoming daily better cultivated and more fully peopled. All places are now accessible, all are well known; most pleasant farms have obliterated all traces of what were once dreary and dangerous wastes; cultivated fields and subdued forests, flocks and herds have expelled wild beasts; sandy deserts are sown; rocks are planted; marshes are drained; and where once were hardly solitary cottages, there are now large cities. No longer are islands dreaded, nor their rocky shores feared; everywhere are houses and inhabitants. Our teeming population is the strongest evidence: our numbers are burdensome to the world, which can hardly supply us from its natural elements; our wants grow more and more keen, and our complaints more bitter in all mouths, whilst Nature fails in affording us her usual sustenance. In every deed, pestilence, and famine and wars, and earthquakes have to be regarded as a remedy for nations, as the means of pruning the luxuriance of the human race.

Tertullian, 337 A.D.